Mariah Carey Qu

CW01508806

101 Questions To Test Your Knowledge
Of This Incredibly Successful Musician

By Colin Carter

Mariah Carey Quiz

This book contains one hundred and one informative
and entertaining trivia questions with multiple choice
answers. With 101 questions, some easy, some more
demanding, this entertaining book will really test
your knowledge of Mariah Carey.

You will be quizzed on a wide range of topics
associated with Mariah Carey for you to test yourself;
with questions on her early days, songs, lyrics,
achievements, awards and much more, guaranteeing
you a truly fun, educational experience.

This quiz book will provide entertainment for fans of
all ages and will certainly test your knowledge of this
world-famous musician. The book is packed with
information and is a must-have for all true Mariah
Carey fans, wherever you live in the world.

Published by Glowworm Press
glowwormpress.com

ACKNOWLEDGEMENTS

I have been a huge fan of Mariah Carey for many years.

As a writer, I thought I would write a book on Mariah Carey for people to see how much they really know about the legend that is Mariah.

So I did! This book is for all you wonderful Mariah Carey fans – wherever you live in the world.

I do hope you enjoy it.

Colin Carter

OK, Let's get started with the first set of questions.

Q1. When was Mariah Carey born?
A) 1969
B) 1970
C) 1971
D) 1972

Q2. What star sign is Mariah?
A) Aries
B) Cancer
C) Capricorn
D) Libra

Q3. Where was Mariah born?
A) Nebraska
B) New Hampshire
C) New Jersey
D) New York

Q4. How many siblings does Mariah have?
A) 1
B) 2
C) 3
D) 4

Q5. What is the name of Mariah's first husband?

A) Mark Sudack

B) Nick Cannon

C) Tommy Mottola

D) Vince Herbert

Q6. When did they marry?
A) 1992
B) 1993
C) 1994
D) 1995

Q7. What is the name of Mariah's second husband?
A) Bryan Tanaka
B) James Packer
C) Nick Cannon
D) Tommy Mottola

Q8. When did they marry?
A) 2005
B) 2006
C) 2007
D) 2008

Q9. Where did they meet?
A) At a concert
D) At a party
C) At a recording studio

B) At a restaurant

Q10. How many children does Mariah have?
A) 1
B) 2
C) 3
D) 4

Here are the answers to the first set of questions.

A1. Mariah Carey was born on March 27, 1969.

A2. Mariah is an Aries. Aries is known for its energetic and enthusiastic traits, which are reflected in her vibrant personality and stage presence.

A3. Mariah was born in Huntington, New York. She began singing at age three, developing her passion for music and performance from an early age.

A4. Mariah has two siblings: an older brother named Morgan and an older sister named Alison. As the youngest, she has experienced both support and challenges in her relationships with her siblings, shaped by their family dynamics.

A5. Mariah's first husband was Tommy Mottola. At the time, he was the head of Sony Music, and their relationship was significant in shaping her early career.

A6. Mariah and Tommy married in 1993. Their marriage was highly publicized due to their professional relationship as well, although it ended in divorce in 1998 due to personal and professional differences.

A7. Mariah's second husband is Nick Cannon. Nick is a prominent figure in the entertainment industry as an actor, comedian, and television host.

A8. Mariah and Nick married in 2008. Their intimate wedding was held on a private island.

A9. Mariah met Nick while filming a music video for her song "Bye Bye." Their connection during the shoot sparked a romantic relationship.

A10. Mariah has two children. They are twins and were born on April 30, 2011. The names of her children carry special meaning, with "Moroccan" inspired by the Moroccan-themed room where Nick Cannon proposed to her, and "Monroe" named after the iconic Marilyn Monroe.

Here is the next set of questions.

Q11. What was Mariah's first job?
A) Barista
B) Flower shop assistant
C) Store clerk
D) Waitress

Q12. What is Mariah's vocal range?
A) Four octaves
B) Five octaves
C) Six octaves
D) Seven octaves

Q13. What color eyes does Mariah have?
A) Amber
B) Dark brown
C) Hazel
D) Light brown

Q14. What color hair does Mariah have?
A) Black
B) Blonde
C) Brown
D) Red

Q15. How tall is Mariah?

A) 5' 6"
B) 5' 7"
C) 5' 8"
D) 5' 9"

Q16. What is Mariah's nickname?
A) The Diva
B) The Emancipator
C) The Queen of Christmas
D) The Songbird Supreme

Q17. What was Mariah's first tattoo?
A) A butterfly
B) A flower
C) A heart
D) A star

Q18. What is Mariah's official website address?
A) careymariah.com
B) mariah.com
C) mariahcarey.com
D) mariahmusic.com

Q19. What is Mariah's official Instagram account?
A) @careymariah
B) @mariah.music
C) @mariahcarey

D) @mariah_carey_official

Q20. What is Mariah's official X (formerly Twitter) account?
A) @carey_mariah
B) @mariah.music
C) @mariahcarey
D) @real_mariah

Here is the latest block of answers.

A11. Mariah's first job was as a waitress. After graduating from Harborfields High School in 1987, she moved to Manhattan and worked as a waitress while pursuing her music career, an experience that helped shape her determination and work ethic.

A12. Mariah is renowned for her five-octave vocal range. This exceptional ability, along with her use of the whistle register, has contributed to her iconic status as one of the greatest vocalists in pop music history.

A13. Mariah has dark brown eyes. Her deep eye color complements her distinctive beauty and has become a recognizable feature of her iconic appearance.

A14. Mariah is known for her naturally curly, dark brown hair. She often styles it in various ways, reflecting her vibrant personality.

A15. Mariah is 5' 9" tall. Her height contributes to her commanding stage presence during performances.

A16. Mariah is often referred to as "The Songbird Supreme." This nickname highlights her extraordinary vocal range and talent as a singer.

A17. Mariah's first tattoo was of a butterfly, which she got on her lower back. The butterfly symbolizes transformation and freedom, resonating with her personal journey.

A18. Mariah's official website is mariahcarey.com. This site features information about her music, tours, and updates on her career.

A19. Mariah's official Instagram account is @mariahcarey. Through this account, she shares updates about her music, personal life, and engages with her fans.

A20. Mariah's official X (formerly Twitter) account is @mariahcarey. She uses this platform to connect with her fans, share updates, and express her thoughts.

Here is the next set of questions.

Q21. What was the name of the first record label Mariah signed to?
A) Atlantic Records
B) Capitol Records
C) Columbia Records
D) Def Jam Recordings

Q22. What is the name of Mariah's first album?
A) Daydream
B) Emotions
C) Mariah Carey
D) Music Box

Q23. When was this debut album released?
A) 1990
B) 1991
C) 1992
D) 1993

Q24. What was the first single Mariah ever released?
A) Dreamlover
B) Hero
C) Music Box
D) Vision of Love

Q25. What is the name of Mariah's second album?

A) Daydream

B) Emotions

C) Glitter

D) Rainbow

Q27. When did Mariah first reach the top of the UK singles chart?

A) 1992

B) 1993

C) 1994

D) 1995

Q28. When did Mariah first reach the top of the US singles chart?

A) 1990

B) 1991

C) 1992

D) 1993

Q29. Which was Mariah's first number one album in the UK?

A) Butterfly

B) Daydream

C) Music Box

D) Rainbow

Q30. Which was Mariah's first number one album in the US?

A) Butterfly

B) Daydream

C) Mariah Carey

D) Music Box

Here is the latest block of answers.

A21. Mariah signed with Columbia Records in 1988. This marked the beginning of her highly successful music career, leading to her breakthrough in the early 1990s.

A22. Mariah's first album is self-titled, "Mariah Carey". The album helped establish her as a major force in the music industry.

A23. Mariah's debut album was released in 1990. It included several hit singles that showcased her extraordinary vocal abilities and laid the foundation for her career.

A24. Mariah's first single was "Vision of Love." It became a major hit and introduced the world to her signature vocal style.

A25. Mariah's second album is titled "Emotions". Released in 1991, it further solidified her reputation as a talented songwriter and vocalist.

A26. As of 2024, Mariah has had 19 number 1 singles on the Billboard Hot 100. This remarkable achievement solidifies her status as one of the most successful solo artists in music history, with may iconic hits leading her to chart-topping success across multiple decades.

A27. Mariah first reached the top of the UK singles chart in 1994 with the song "Without You." This became a massive hit, earning her widespread international acclaim.

A28. Mariah first topped the US singles chart in 1990 with "Vision of Love." The song's success introduced her to a global audience and kick-started her extraordinary career.

A29. Mariah's first number one album in the UK was Music Box, debuting in September 1993.

A30. Mariah's first number one album in the US was her self-titled debut, "Mariah Carey". It topped the charts in 1991, following the success of her breakout singles.

OK, let's have some music video related questions.

Q31. Who directed the music video for "Honey"?
A) Brett Ratner
B) David LaChapelle
C) Hype Williams
D) Paul Hunter

Q32. Where was the music video for "My All" filmed?
A) Greece
B) Italy
C) Puerto Rico
D) Spain

Q33. Which of Mariah's music videos features a carnival theme?
A) Dreamlover
B) Fantasy
C) Hero
D) I'll Be There

Q34. What music video shows Mariah in a boxing ring?
A) Breakdown
B) Butterfly
C) Heartbreaker
D) Vision of Love

Q35. In which music video does Mariah play a secret agent?

A) Always Be My Baby

B) Honey

C) One Sweet Day

D) Without You

Q36. Who directed the music video for "We Belong Together"?

A) Benny Boom

B) Brett Ratner

C) David LaChapelle

D) Francis Lawrence

Q37. What music video features Mariah in a wedding dress?

A) Against All Odds

B) Love Takes Time

C) Thank God I Found You

D) We Belong Together

Q38. Which music video features Mariah riding a horse?

A) Butterfly

B) I Still Believe

C) Music Box

D) My All

Q39. Which music video shows Mariah as a mermaid?

A) Bliss

B) Emotions

C) Underneath the Stars

D) You're Mine

Q40. Where was the music video for "Dreamlover" filmed?

A) Copake, New York

B) Greenwich, Connecticut

C) Miami, Florida

D) Santa Monica, California

Here are the answers to the music video questions.

A31. The music video for "Honey" was directed by Paul Hunter. This video featured Mariah in an adventurous, James Bond-inspired storyline.

A32. The music video for "My All" was filmed in Puerto Rico. Shot entirely in black and white, the video was directed by fashion photographer Herb Ritts, giving it a timeless, elegant look.

A33. The music video for "Fantasy" features a carnival theme. Set at an amusement park, Mariah roller-skates and enjoys the vibrant atmosphere, reflecting the song's joyful energy.

A34. Mariah appears in a boxing ring in the "Heartbreaker" music video. The video, directed by Brett Ratner, features a fight scene between two versions of Mariah in a movie theater.

A35. Mariah plays a secret agent in the "Honey" music video. The video is full of action-packed sequences and was a turning point in her career, marking her more independent and empowered image.

A36. Brett Ratner directed the music video for "We Belong Together." This video features Mariah escaping her wedding and reconnecting with her true love.

A37. The music video for "We Belong Together" shows Mariah in a wedding dress. The storyline follows her as she decides to leave the wedding for her true love.

A38. The "Butterfly" music video features Mariah riding a horse, symbolizing freedom and grace. This imagery enhances the song's themes of transformation and liberation, adding a whimsical and dreamlike quality to the visual experience.

A39. Mariah appears as a mermaid in the music video for "You're Mine (Eternal)." The video showcases scenes of her covered in gold glitter beside a river, swimming underwater in an evening gown, and surrounded by tropical wildlife in El Yunque National Forest, Puerto Rico.

A40. The music video for "Dreamlover" was filmed in the countryside of Copake, New York. It opens with underwater swimming scenes, followed by Mariah in a green field, wearing short jeans and a knotted t-shirt, while a group of young dancers perform in the grass around her.

Let's have some lyrics related questions.

Q41. Which song starts with the lyrics, "I need a lover to give me the kind of love that'll last always."?
A) Dreamlover
B) Emotions
C) Just to Hold You Once Again
D) Without You

Q42. Which song starts with the lyrics, "There's a hero if you look inside your heart"?
A) Against All Odds
B) Hero
C) I Don't Wanna Cry
D) Vision Of Love

Q43. Which song starts with the lyrics, "If you're lonely and need a friend"?
A) Anytime You Need a Friend
B) I'll Be There
C) Never Forget You
D) Someday

Q44. Which song starts with the lyrics, "When I am lost you shine a light for me and set me free"?
A) Close My Eyes
B) Endless Love
C) Music Box

D) Underneath the Stars

Q45. Which song starts with the lyrics, "Sorry I never told you, all I wanted to say"?
A) I Don't Wanna Cry
B) Love Takes Time
C) My All
D) One Sweet Day

Q46. Which song starts with the lyrics, "Treated me kind, sweet destiny"?
A) Butterfly
B) Can't Take That Away
C) Heartbreaker
D) Vision Of Love

Q47. Which song starts with the lyrics, "You were so blind to let me go"?
A) Can't Let Go
B) Close My Eyes
C) Now That I Know
D) Someday

Q48. Which song starts with the lyrics, "I had it all, but I let it slip away"?
A) Bliss
B) I Still Believe
C) Love Takes Time

D) Make It Happen

Q49. Which song starts with the lyrics, "They can say anything they want to say try to bring me down"?
A) Can't Take That Away
B) Forever
C) I Don't Wanna Cry
D) When You Believe

Q50. Which song starts with the lyrics, "I would give up everything before I'd separate myself from you"?
A) All I've Ever Wanted
B) Bliss
C) Honey
D) Thank God I Found You

Here are the answers to the lyrics questions.

A41. "Dreamlover" starts with the lyrics "I need a lover to give me the kind of love that'll last always." This opening expresses a longing for love and companionship that drives the song's romantic theme.

A42. "Hero" begins with the lyrics "There's a hero if you look inside your heart." This powerful opening sets the stage for a song about finding strength within oneself.

A43. "Anytime You Need a Friend" starts with the lyrics "When you're lost in the darkness, and you can't see the light." This line conveys a message of support and assurance in times of trouble.

A44. "Music Box" starts with the lyrics "When I am lost you shine a light for me and set me free." This powerful opening beautifully captures the theme of love as a guiding force that brings freedom and clarity in times of uncertainty.

A45. "One Sweet Day" starts with the lyrics "Sorry I never told you, all I wanted to say." This poignant opening conveys feelings of regret and longing, establishing the song's heartfelt tribute to lost loved ones.

A46. "Vision of Love" begins with the lyrics "Treated me kind, sweet destiny." This opening line expresses gratitude and hope, reflecting the song's overarching theme of yearning for a deep and meaningful connection.

A47. "Someday" begins with the lyrics "You were so blind to let me go." This opening line reflects themes of nostalgia and the enduring nature of love.

A48. "Love Takes Time" begins with the lyrics "I had it all, but I let it slip away." This line evokes a deep sense of loss and longing, highlighting the fragile nature of love and relationships.

A49. "Can't Take That Away" starts with the lyrics "They can say anything they want to say try to bring me down." This opening conveys a powerful message of resilience and strength in the face of adversity, emphasizing the importance of self-acceptance and love.

A50. "Thank God I Found You" begins with the lyrics "I would give up everything/Before I'd separate myself from you." This line emphasizes the profound commitment to love and the lengths one would go to maintain a cherished relationship.

Here are some album-related questions.

Q51. Which album includes the song "Always Be My Baby"?
A) Charmbracelet
B) Daydream
C) Emotions
D) Music Box

Q52. Which album includes the song "Honey"?
A) Butterfly
B) Charmbracelet
C) Daydream
D) Glitter?

Q53. Which album features the hit single "Vision of Love"?
A) Emotions
B) Mariah Carey
C) Merry Christmas
D) Rainbow

Q54. Which album includes the song "Heartbreaker"?
A) Charmbracelet
B) Glitter
C) Rainbow
D) The Emancipation of Mimi

Q55. Which album includes "O Holy Night"?
A) All I Want for Christmas Is You
B) Merry Christmas
C) Merry Christmas II You
D) Santa Claus Is Coming to Town

Q56. Which album features the song "Obsessed"?
A) Charmbracelet
B) E=MC²
C) Memoirs of an Imperfect Angel
D) The Emancipation of Mimi

Q57. Which album includes the song "My All"?
A) Butterfly
B) Daydream
C) Emotions
D) Music Box

Q58. Which album features the hit single "We Belong Together"?
A) Emotions
B) Glitter
C) Rainbow
D) The Emancipation of Mimi

Q59. Which album includes the song "Hero"?
A) Daydream
B) Emotions

C) Mariah Carey

D) Music Box

Q60. Which album features "Lullaby"?

A) Charmbracelet

B) Mariah Carey

C) Memoirs of an Imperfect Angel

D) Rainbow

Here are the answers to the latest set of questions.

A51. "Always Be My Baby" is a single from the studio album, "Daydream," released in March 1996. This hit showcases Mariah's signature blend of pop and R&B, emphasizing themes of love and longing, and has become one of her most iconic tracks.

A52. "Honey" is included in the album "Butterfly". This song marked a shift in Mariah's musical style, incorporating elements of hip-hop and dance, and it became one of her most successful singles.

A53. "Mariah Carey" features the hit single "Vision of Love." This debut single not only launched Mariah's career but also showcased her impressive vocal range and songwriting ability, establishing her as a leading figure in the music industry.

A54. "Rainbow" includes the song "Heartbreaker." This collaboration with Jay-Z is notable for its catchy hook and rap interlude, blending pop and hip-hop and demonstrating Mariah's versatility as an artist.

A55. Mariah covered the traditional Christmas song "O Holy Night" for her 1994 Merry Christmas album. This album became a classic holiday release.

A56. "Memoirs of an Imperfect Angel" features the song "Obsessed." This track showcases Mariah's vocal prowess and witty lyrics, addressing themes of love and obsession, and it became a commercial success.

A57. "Butterfly" includes the song "My All." This emotional ballad highlights Mariah's incredible vocal range and vulnerability, capturing the essence of longing and love.

A58. "The Emancipation of Mimi" features the hit single "We Belong Together." This song marked a significant comeback for Mariah, showcasing her vocal ability and emotional depth, and it received critical acclaim.

A59. "Music Box" includes the song "Hero." This inspirational anthem has resonated with fans worldwide, emphasizing themes of strength and resilience, and is one of Mariah's most beloved tracks.

A60. "Lullaby" is featured in the album Charmbracelet. This album highlights Mariah's intimate and reflective songwriting, offering a more subdued and emotional side of her music.

Here is the next set of questions.

Q61. Who was the producer of Mariah's best-selling album "Music Box"?
A) David Foster
B) Ric Wake
C) Tommy Mottola
D) Walter Afanasieff

Q62. Who was the producer of "The Emancipation of Mimi"?
A) Bryan-Michael Cox
B) Jermaine Dupri
C) Timbaland
D) Tommy Mottola

Q63. Who did Mariah collaborate with on the song "When You Believe"?
A) Barbra Streisand
B) Celine Dion
C) Toni Braxton
D) Whitney Houston

Q64. Who sang with Mariah on the song "Endless Love"?
A) Brian McKnight
B) Elton John
C) Luther Vandross

D) Stevie Wonder

Q65. Who did Mariah team up with for the song "One Sweet Day"?
A) Backstreet Boys
B) Boyz II Men
C) NSYNC
D) 98 Degrees

Q66. Who sang with Mariah on the song "Against All Odds (Take a Look at Me Now)"?
A) A1
B) Blue
C) Five
D) Westlife

Q67. Who sang with Mariah on the song "I Know What You Want"?
A) Busta Rhymes
B) Jay-Z
C) Nas
D) Snoop Dogg

Q68. Who sang with Mariah on the song "Thank God I Found You"?
A) Backstreet Boys
B) Five
C) Joe & 98 Degrees

D) NSYNC

Q69. Who sang with Mariah on the song "Angels Cry"?
A) Bruno Mars
B) Chris Brown
C) Ne-Yo
D) Usher

Q70. Who sang with Mariah on the song "Up Out My Face"?
A) Beyoncé
B) Cardi B
C) Jennifer Lopez
D) Nicki Minaj

Here are the answers to the latest block of questions.

A61. The producer of Mariah's best-selling album "Music Box" was Walter Afanasieff. His collaboration with Mariah on this album resulted in several chart-topping hits, showcasing their synergy and creative chemistry.

A62. The producer of "The Emancipation of Mimi" was Jermaine Dupri. His influence on the album helped blend hip-hop and R&B elements, contributing to its commercial success and critical acclaim.

A63. Mariah collaborated with Whitney Houston on the song "When You Believe." This powerful duet, featured in the animated film "The Prince of Egypt," showcases the vocal prowess of both artists and became a significant hit.

A64. Mariah collaborated with Luther Vandross on the song "Endless Love." This heartfelt duet, originally performed by Diana Ross and Lionel Richie, was featured on Luther's 1994 album Songs.

A65. Mariah teamed up with Boyz II Men for the song "One Sweet Day." This powerful ballad became one of the longest-running number one hits in Billboard history, touching on themes of loss and remembrance.

A66. Mariah collaborated with Westlife on the 2000 version of "Against All Odds (Take a Look at Me Now)," originally by Phil Collins. Their version was a hit in the UK and other parts of Europe.

A67. Mariah teamed up with Busta Rhymes on "I Know What You Want," a hit single from Busta's album It Ain't Safe No More. The song's catchy hook made it a fan favorite.

A68. Mariah collaborated with Joe and 98 Degrees on "Thank God I Found You," a soulful ballad from her album Rainbow, which topped the Billboard Hot 100.

A69. Mariah collaborated with Ne-Yo on the song "Angels Cry." The emotional duet blends their powerful vocals, adding depth to the heartfelt ballad.

A70. Mariah collaborated with Nicki Minaj on the song "Up Out My Face," from her album Memoirs of an Imperfect Angel. Their dynamic partnership added an edgy vibe to the track.

Here is the next set of questions.

Q71. What is the title of Mariah's autobiography?
A) All I Want for Christmas Is You
B) Butterfly: The Memoir
C) Mariah: The Autobiography
D) The Meaning of Mariah Carey

Q72. Which item of Marilyn Monroe's does Mariah own?
A) Diamond necklace
B) Fur coat
C) Gold bracelet
D) White baby grand piano

Q73. Which Mariah song is known for its iconic whistle note?
A) Always Be My Baby
B) Emotions
C) My All
D) We Belong Together

Q74. What is Mariah's signature holiday song?
A) All I Want for Christmas Is You
B) Hark! The Herald Angels Sing
C) O Holy Night
D) Silent Night

Q75. In which movie did Mariah play the role of a social worker named Mrs. Weiss?
A) Glitter
B) Precious
C) Tennessee
D) The Butler

Q76. On which reality TV show did Mariah join as a judge for its twelfth season?
A) American Idol
B) America's Got Talent
C) The Voice
D) The X Factor

Q77. If Mariah were classified as an opera singer, what voice category would she fall under?
A) Contralto
B) Coloratura soprano
C) Lyric soprano
D) Mezzo soprano

Q78. Who did Mariah sing backing vocals for before her big break?
A) Brenda K. Starr
B) Celine Dion
C) Janet Jackson
D) Whitney Houston

Q79. Which Las Vegas Hotel did Mariah have a residency at in 2024 & 2025?

A) Bellagio

B) Caesars Palace

C) Mandalay Bay

D) Park MGM

Q80. Which of her films did Mariah disown after it was a critical and financial failure?

A) Glitter

B) Precious

C) The Butler

D) WiseGirls

Here is the latest set of answers.

A71. Mariah's autobiography is titled "The Meaning of Mariah Carey." Published in 2020, the book provides a deep and personal insight into her life, career, and the challenges she has faced throughout her journey in the music industry.

A72. Mariah owns Marilyn Monroe's white baby grand piano, which originally belonged to Monroe's mother. She purchased it for $662,500 in 1999, reflecting her admiration for the iconic actress.

A73. The song "Emotions" is known for its iconic whistle notes. Mariah's ability to reach these high notes in the track showcases her extraordinary vocal talent and has become a defining characteristic of her musical style.

A74. Mariah's signature holiday song is "All I Want for Christmas Is You." The track has become a Christmas classic and is one of the best-selling holiday songs of all time, showcasing her vocal prowess and catchy songwriting.

A75. Mariah played the role of Mrs. Weiss, a social worker, in the critically acclaimed film Precious. Her understated performance was praised for its depth and departure from her glamorous persona.

A76. Mariah joined the judging panel of American Idol for its twelfth season. Her presence brought star power and experience to the popular TV show.

A77. Mariah would be classified as a coloratura soprano if she were an opera singer. This category encompasses a wide vocal range and the ability to perform intricate melodies, reflecting her impressive vocal capabilities.

A78. Mariah provided backing vocals for Brenda K. Starr before achieving her own success. This experience helped her gain exposure in the music industry and paved the way for her eventual rise to stardom.

A79. Mariah performed her 2024 & 2025 Las Vegas residency at Dolby Live at Park MGM, to sell-out crowds. This residency showcased her greatest hits with captivating performances for her fans.

A80. Mariah disowned her 2001 film Glitter after it received poor reviews and failed at the box office. Despite this, the movie later gained a cult following among her fans.

Here is the next set of questions.

Q81. What song contains the lyrics, "Whenever you call, I'll be there"?
A) Anytime You Need a Friend
B) Hero
C) I Still Believe
D) Whenever You Call

Q82. What song contains the lyrics, "Believe me I'm not pretending, it's not hard to predict"?
A) Always Be My Baby
B) Honey
C) Someday
D) Thank God I Found You

Q83. What song contains the lyrics, "With an unselfish love I'll respect you"?
A) Butterfly
C) I'll Be There
B) Love Takes Time
D) Without You

Q84. What song contains the lyrics, "If you search within yourself, and the emptiness you felt will disappear"?
A) Against All Odds
B) Emotions

C) Fantasy

D) Hero

Q85. The lyrics, "You'll always be a part of me, I'm part of you indefinitely" is from what song?

A) Always Be My Baby

B) Dreamlover

C) Heartbreaker

D) Obsessed

Q86. What song includes the lyrics, "Talkin' sweet and lookin' fine, I get kinda hectic inside"?

A) Fantasy

B) Music Box

C) My All

D) Vision of Love

Q87. What song has the lyrics, "Cause it's blatant that I'm feeling you"?

A) Endless Love

B) Honey

C) Sweetheart

D) We Belong Together

Q88. What song includes the line, "Never had I imagined living without your smile"?

A) I Don't Wanna Cry

B) Love Takes Time

C) One Sweet Day

D) Without You

Q89. What song contains the lyrics, "I don't want a pretender to delusion me one more time"?

A) Dreamlover

B) Touch My Body

C) Vision of Love

D) When You Believe

Q90. What song contains the lyrics, "When you love me tenderly, I don't know if you're for real"?

A) Angels Cry

B) Emotions

C) Endless Love

D) We Belong Together

Here are the answers to the last set of questions

A81. The lyrics "Whenever you call, I'll be there" are from "Whenever You Call." This song showcases Mariah's vocal prowess and emotional depth, emphasizing themes of support and love.

A82. The lyrics "Believe me I'm not pretending, it's not hard to predict" are from "Someday." This song expresses themes of longing and heartbreak, showcasing Mariah's emotional depth and vocal prowess.

A83. The lyrics "With an unselfish love I'll respect you" are from "I'll Be There." This heartfelt ballad showcases themes of unconditional love and support, making it one of Mariah's most cherished songs.

A84. The lyrics "If you search within yourself, and the emptiness you felt will disappear" are from "Hero." The song inspires hope and inner strength, resonating with listeners around the world.

A85. The lyrics "You'll always be a part of me, I'm part of you indefinitely" are from "Always Be My Baby." This song emphasizes an unbreakable bond between lovers, showcasing Mariah's distinctive sound.

A86. The lyrics "Talkin' sweet and lookin' fine, I get kinda hectic inside" are from "Fantasy." This upbeat track showcases Mariah's signature blend of pop and R&B, highlighting her infectious energy and vocal style.

A87. The lyrics "Cause it's blatant that I'm feeling you" are from "Honey." This catchy song features a hip-hop remix, which helped propel it to the top of the charts.

A88. The lyrics "Never had I imagined living without your smile" are from "One Sweet Day." This poignant song topped the Billboard Hot 100 chart for 16 consecutive weeks, making it one of the longest-running number one songs in history.

A89. The lyrics "I don't want a pretender to delusion me one more time" are from "Dreamlover." This upbeat track showcases Mariah's vibrant energy and longing for genuine love and connection.

A90. The lyrics "When you love me tenderly, I don't know if you're for real" are from "Emotions." This upbeat track combines joy and uncertainty, showcasing Mariah's range and vocal power.

Here's the final set of questions.

Q91. How many Grammy Awards has Mariah won?
A) 3
B) 4
C) 5
D) 6

Q92. Which year did Mariah win her first Grammy Award?
A) 1990
B) 1991
C) 1992
D) 1993

Q93. What honor did Mariah receive in 2015?
A) Billboard Icon Award
B) Grammy Lifetime Achievement Award
C) Kennedy Center Honor
D) Star on the Hollywood Walk of Fame

Q94. What is Mariah's best-selling single of all time?
A) All I Want for Christmas Is You
B) Always Be My Baby
C) One Sweet Day
D) We Belong Together

Q95. What event featured Mariah's "stunning" rendition of "The Star-Spangled Banner," as described by Billboard?

A) The Academy Awards

B) The Grammy Awards

C) The MTV Video Music Awards

D) Super Bowl XXXVI

Q96.How many records has Mariah sold, making her one of the best-selling recording artists in history?

A) 50 million

B) 100 million

C) 150 million

D) 200 million

Q97. When did Mariah sing during Carpool Karaoke?

A) 2014

B) 2015

C) 2016

D) 2017

Q98. Which part of Mariah's body is insured for $1 billion?

A) Arms

B) Hair

C) Legs

D) Voice

Q99. At which benefit concert did Mariah perform in dedication to the victims and heroes of the World Trade Center tragedy?

A) 9/11 Memorial Concert

B) A Day of Remembrance

C) A Tribute to Heroes

D) The Concert for New York City

Q100. How many songs does Mariah have that reached #1 on the US Billboard Hot 100 charts?

A) 15

B) 16

C) 17

D) 18

Q101. What are Mariah's fans called?

A) Carey's Crew

B) Lambs

C) Mariah's Angels

D) Mariah's Friends

Here are the answers to the final set of questions.

A91. Mariah has won five Grammy Awards throughout her career. Her wins reflect her significant contributions to the music industry and her incredible vocal talent.

A92. Mariah won her first two Grammy Awards at the 33rd Grammy Awards in 1991, including Best New Artist. This milestone marked the beginning of her illustrious career and solidified her as a powerful presence in the music industry.

A93. In 2015, Mariah received a Star on the Hollywood Walk of Fame in the Recording category, celebrating her immense contributions to the music industry and her legacy as one of the best-selling artists of all time.

A94. Mariah's best-selling single of all time is "All I Want for Christmas Is You." Released in 1994, the song has become a holiday classic and continues to top charts every Christmas season, showcasing Mariah's lasting impact on pop culture.

A95. Mariah delivered her "stunning" rendition of "The Star-Spangled Banner" at Super Bowl XXXVI. Her performance was widely praised and highlighted her vocal prowess on a significant national stage.

A96. Mariah has sold more than 220 million records worldwide, establishing her as one of the best-selling recording artists in history. This impressive achievement underscores her global influence and longevity in the music industry.

A97. Mariah sang during Carpool Karaoke in 2015, on The Late Late Show with James Corden. Initially hesitant, she eventually joined in, creating a memorable moment for fans.

A98. Mariah insured her legs for $1 billion when she was chosen for Gillette's "Legs of a Goddess" campaign. This extravagant move highlights her iconic status and the value placed on her image in the entertainment industry.

A99. Mariah performed "Hero" at the benefit concert "A Tribute to Heroes" in September 2001, honoring the families, friends, and victims of the World Trade Center tragedy. This emotional performance showcased her commitment to supporting those affected by the events of that day.

A100. Mariah has 18 #1 songs on the US Billboard Hot 100 charts, making her the only female artist to achieve this remarkable milestone. This accomplishment highlights her incredible impact on the music industry.

A101. Mariah's fans are affectionately known as "Lambs." This term reflects the close and loyal relationship she shares with her fanbase, who support her music and career passionately.

That's a great question to finish with.

That's it. I hope you enjoyed this book, and I hope you got most of the answers right. I also hope you learnt some new things about Mariah!

If you have any comments or if you saw anything wrong, please email support@glowwormpress.com and we'll get the book updated. We have updated the book thanks to other Mariah Carey fans, and we do read every email.

There is just one thing left to do and that's to leave a positive review on Amazon saying what you think of Mariah Carey.

Many thanks in advance.

Printed in Dunstable, United Kingdom

65607728R00037